Adventures in Science and Mathematics

Integrated Activities for Young Children

Julie Gordon Whitney & Linda Jensen Sheffield

Cuisenaire Company of America, Inc.

Cover: Arthur Celedonia

Design: CIRCA 86, Inc.

Copyright © 1991 by Cuisenaire Company of America, Inc.
10 Bank Street, P.O. Box 5026, White Plains, New York 10602-5026

ISBN 0-938587-18-8

1 2 3 4 5 6 7 8 9 10-FC-96959493

Table of Contents

Introduction

Science is not the art of memorizing facts and mathematics does not mean counting to ten. Science and math are much more than that; they are the processes of seeking new knowledge and understanding the world around us. The National Council of Teachers of Mathematics (NCTM) has developed the *Curriculum and Evaluation Standards for School Mathematics* for kindergarten through high school. The American Association for the Advancement of Science (AAAS) in their report *2061* also have developed a set of recommendations for teaching science in kindergarten through twelfth grade. These reports both stress "hands-on" activities and the importance of integrating science and mathematics instruction at all levels.

Adventures In Science and Math has been written to help you implement these guidelines in your classroom. All of the activities in this book are designed to be participative and to provide immediate results, so that students retain a high level of interest throughout.

The activities are all based on experiences in the physical sciences. These experiences are the most basic part of a child's world, and include movement, rolling, sliding, waterplay, and perception of light and color. At the same time, any exploration into the physical sciences is linked inseparably to such mathematical experiences as classifying, measuring, and comparing.

Each of the five units of the book begins by giving an overview and background information about each activity so that teachers can feel comfortable with the material being presented. The materials required for each activity are identified, and instructions and illustrations are given to help you to set up the experiments. Many of the materials you will need for the activities may already be in your classroom. Others are readily available.

Every activity is designed to follow basically the same process; this reinforces the scientific method: experiment and observe, discuss, hypothesize, test hypotheses, discuss results, and explore further. Every exploration encourages communication, reasoning, and problem solving as students explore how things work. To support this, students should be asked to reflect on what happened by drawing pictures or writing one or two summary statements.

The activities are designed to be used by students as young as three or four years old with adult supervision and with students as old as second graders on a more independent basis. You will be able to choose the level of activity most suited to your students.

Most activities can be done as a combination of small group or paired experimentation and whole class discussion. Alternatively, you may wish to set up certain activities in learning centers.

Learning About the World

The activities in this unit introduce students to the scientific method, which they will use as they engage in each of the activities in this book. The scientific method is a process by which we investigate and learn about our world. It involves observing, gathering and organizing information, forming tentative ideas, planning and carrying out experiments, and drawing conclusions. The information that we gain through the scientific method is less important than the process by which we gather that information. The reason for this is simple: what we think we know is subject to change at any time, as new evidence becomes available. The only thing that is constant is the method by which we evaluate the new evidence and new theories.

The process of scientific investigation begins with making observations. Observations serve as the basis for all knowledge, because it is from careful observations that hypotheses, or tentative theories, are made. We make observations by gathering information about the world with all of our senses. Scientific observation is never a passive event. To learn from an observation, we need to classify and organize what is being observed. Sequencing, sorting, classifying, comparing, and measuring all help us to see relationships or patterns. These patterns point to hypotheses about why things are happening. In fact, sometimes the only clue as to what is really happening may come from classifying and organizing observable information.

We test a hypothesis by experimenting. In an experiment, we control the surroundings of a particular event. The outcome of the experiment may confirm what we suspected or it may rule out a possibility. In science, a single experiment is seldom enough to prove anything, so experiments are often repeated to confirm initial results. Frequently, experiments have unexpected outcomes. When this happens, scientists are sent scrambling for new explanations and new theories. Then the process starts all over again.

The setting for this investigation into the scientific process will be the study of rocks. Scientists study rocks for several compelling reasons. For one thing, different kinds of rocks were formed in different ways and each tells a story of the history of an area. Scientists use this information to describe what the earth was like millions of years ago. Geologists study rocks for clues as to what valuable minerals or other resources might be buried beneath us. Meteorologists study the structure of certain rocks to help predict earthquakes. Children, too, can find rocks a wonderful subject for investigation. Readily available, rocks also have many attributes which can be observed, measured, and sequenced. Among these are color, size, structure, hardness, and density. Children can also describe rocks according to their various uses. For example, salt is edible, while coal may be burned for fuel.

The first activity in this unit involves making simple observations. Students go on "field trips" to collect rocks, some of which they will examine and describe. In the second activity, students make predictions about rocks based on their observations, then verify them through more careful investigation. In the third activity, students work with various tools (screens or strainers, bowls of water, and magnifying glasses) to make further discoveries about rocks (and pebbles). The fourth activity involves performing scratch tests to sequence students' rocks from hardest to softest. The factors that make some rocks hard and others soft have to do with structure and forces. Rocks, like everything else around us, act according to the physical laws of nature. In Unit Two, students will begin to look at these physical laws by examining forces.

Making Simple
Observations and Comparisons

OVERVIEW

Observational skills are important both for mathematical and scientific inquiry. Since observation is such an integral part of their everyday lives, it is easy for some students to believe that they have fulfilled the task at hand when they have observed only briefly. They can know that the sun is shining by seeing it and by feeling its warmth. They can observe that the stereo is on by hearing it or by feeling the vibrations in the speakers. But real observational skills do not stop with first impressions.

This activity requires students to go beyond the first quick observation. Students begin by sharing whatever information they already may have about rocks. In this way, you can get an idea of each student's level of understanding. Students then collect rocks and observe their color, shape, size, feel, weight, and hardness. Next, students compare their observations of two rocks. Students can use these comparisons to organize and sort rocks into various groupings. Thus, students begin to learn some of the most basic scientific and mathematical processes: observing, comparing, and classifying.

Three types of rocks which students may find are sedimentary, metamorphic, and igneous. *Sedimentary* rocks were formed when dust, seashells, and sand settled to the bottom of ancient lakes and oceans in layers called *sediment*. Over time, the layers hardened into sedimentary rock. Three types of sedimentary rock are sandstone, which is made of grains of sand pressed together; shale, which is made of mud and clay pressed together; and limestone, which is made of shells pressed together. *Metamorphic* rocks are rocks which have changed over time from one kind of rock to another. For example, marble was once limestone, quartzite was formed from sandstone, and slate evolved from shale. *Igneous* rocks are those which have melted and rehardened. Granite and the volcanic rocks basalt, obsidian, and pumice are examples of igneous rocks. Although some children may find this information of interest, none of the activities in this unit require the identification of rocks.

MATERIALS

For each student:

- a wide variety of rocks
- a box or bag for collecting rocks
- the book *The Magic School Bus Inside the Earth* (optional)

ACTIVITY

Begin with a general discussion about rocks. To help students appreciate what they already know, you might want to ask such questions as: *What are rocks? Where do you see rocks? What are rocks like? What color rocks have you seen? Where was the biggest rock you have ever* seen? Where do rocks come from? What are rocks good for? Are bricks or concrete rocks? This discussion serves several purposes. Every young child has some experience of rocks, so everyone should have something to share. Sharing observations with a group can help increase students' interest and self confidence. Talking about what is and what isn't a rock will stimulate curiosity. Talking about color, size, and other properties may help students become more aware as they begin to observe.

Students can collect rocks over the course of several days. Begin by taking students outside into a schoolyard or a backyard, or beside a road, where they can collect their first rocks. After that, you might take students on other outings to different locations near the school. Students may also want to bring rocks from home. As rocks are gathered, they should be kept together in each student's rock bag or box. A good rock collection should have five to ten rocks, including at least three different kind of rocks.

Ask each student to choose one rock to share with the class. The student should describe as many properties of the rock as possible. Encourage students to use all their senses in talking about such properties as size, shape, feel, color, weight, and smell. (You may want to warn students against tasting the rocks.) After students have described one rock, ask each of them to pick two other rocks and describe how they are alike and how they are different. You might extend this with a game in which everyone sits in a circle. One student begins by picking out a rock and describing it. The next student chooses another rock and tells at least one way in which it is like the first rock. Later, you can vary the activity by asking the students to choose a rock that is different in at least one way.

Encourage students to record the activity by drawing two or more rocks and writing down some of their observations. Be sure that students include how the rocks are alike and how the rocks are different. Younger children may need to dictate their observations.

FURTHER EXPLORATION

Ask students to group their rocks in as many different ways as possible. First and second grade students can form small groups and play a game in which one person sorts rocks according to some criterion, and the others attempt to guess how the rocks were sorted. The student who guesses then gets to sort the rocks next.

The book *The Magic School Bus Inside the Earth* (Cole, 1987) is an excellent way to end the activity for students in the early grades. The book is a humorous story about a class that goes on a journey through the earth to collect rocks.

Using Observations to Make Inferences

OVERVIEW

Making inferences based on observable facts is essential both in everyday living and for scientific investigation. But observations do not always lead to valid inferences. Take an example from ordinary experience. We view a picture of a girl with tears streaming down her face and correctly observe that she is crying. We may then infer that the girl is sad. But, since people sometimes cry because they are intensely happy, relieved, or deeply moved, our inference might not be right. To discover why the girl is crying, we would need to investigate further. Or consider an example from the world of science. Suppose a scientist who seeks a cure for cancer gives an experimental drug to an ailing rat. Say the cancer quickly disappears, but the rat soon gets pneumonia and dies. If the scientist immediately infers that the rat died either of the cancer or of the medicine, the scientist might decide that the new drug is unsuccessful, even though it actually worked. For a scientist, such an incorrect inference can be a serious problem, because it is likely to misdirect further investigation. Fortunately, in the case of the dead rat, an actual scientist would probably examine the dead rat for evidence of the presence or absence of cancer cells before making an inference about the experiment.

When students make predictions based on their observations, these predictions are the result of inferences that students have drawn. In this activity, for example, students will observe pairs of rocks of different sizes. Before holding the rocks, students may infer that the larger rock must be the heavier. But, by checking their weight predictions through experimentation, students will be able to see that size and weight are not necessarily related.

MATERIALS

- a variety of types and sizes of rocks, at least ten pieces labeled a, b, c, and so on
- a pan balance
- "fake" rocks (optional)

ACTIVITY

Begin by showing students two rocks of the same type (for example, sandstone), but of different sizes, which you have labeled with letters. Ask students first to describe the rocks, and then predict which one will prove to be heavier. After students talk about how they arrived at their predictions, ask them how they can quickly get more information about which rock is heavier. Then give various students a chance to hold the two rocks, one in each hand, and observe their relative weight.

Point out that a scale gives more exact information about weight than a person can make by holding an object and guessing. Explain that a pan balance is a kind of scale. Invite students to describe what happens when something is placed on a pan balance. Then put one rock on one side of the balance and have students observe and discuss what happens. Ask: *What would happen if there were two rocks of the same weight one on each side of the balance? What if there were two rocks of different weight on the balance?* Finally, have students predict what will happen when you place each of the remaining labeled rocks on the balance. Call on a volunteer to verify these predictions by placing the rocks on the balance. Encourage students to compare this result with their original predictions and to discuss what they learned.

After students have made observations and predictions about rocks of the same type, show them two rocks of different sizes and types. (A small heavy rock such as granite and a larger lightweight rock such as pumice would work well here.) Again, ask students first to predict which rock is heavier without picking up the rocks. Then let students verify their predictions by lifting the rocks. Ask whether students' judgments change after they use their sense of touch or feel to make additional observations. Let students use the balance scale to determine more exactly which rock is heavier. Have students compare their predictions with their findings and share their ideas about what they learned.

FURTHER EXPLORATION

This activity can be extended with a variety of artificial rocks, which will be lighter than they appear to be. "Fake" rocks are available in the gift shops of many natural history museums. Students can also use a light material such as styrofoam, which comes in various shapes, and can be purchased from craft stores.

Making Observations Using Tools

OVERVIEW

Simple tools such as scales, magnifying glasses, and even strainers can help students to take a second look and make better observations. Tools aid our senses by enhancing the features we need to observe. Tools also help to quantify things. If a person says a rock is heavy, you know less than if they say it weighs three pounds.

This is a three-part activity. First students use filters (screens or strainers) to separate and distinguish sand from gravel. Next, they use water as a tool for finding the volume of the rocks. Last, they use a magnifying glass to examine crystal structures.

MATERIALS

- pieces of screen, or strainers
- a mixture of sand and gravel
- large paper plates
- rocks of different types and sizes from students' rock collections
- clear plastic glasses, filled halfway with water
- markers or crayons that can mark on glass
- measuring cup (optional)
- magnifying glasses
- masking tape
- salt
- sand
- rock candy
- pan balance
- sugar (optional)
- string (optional)
- empty jars (optional)
- pencils (optional)
- paper clips (optional)

ACTIVITY

Using a Screen to Sort First, have students form small groups, then distribute mounds of gravel mixed with sand to each group. Have students take a good look at their mound of gravel and sand to determine which there is more of, sand or gravel. Ask why it is hard to tell. Then have students try to sort out the gravel from the sand by hand. Encourage students to talk about what they are experiencing. Ask: *Is this a fast way to do the job? Are you sure you can get all the gravel? Is there a better way to do this?*

Give each group a piece of screen, or a strainer. Ask: *How could this tool help you with the problem of finding out whether there is more gravel or sand?* Let students use their screen or strainer to separate the gravel and the sand into two piles. Ask: *Which way of sorting was easier* and faster, by hand or with the screen (or strainer)? Now have students identify the larger pile. (This can be confirmed by using a small measuring cup.) Then ask them which pile is heavier, and why. Have them check to see if they are right, by weighing the two piles on a pan balance. Ask: *Is the heavier pile also the larger pile?*

Finding the Volume in Water Have students look at their rock collections and select two rocks that are of similar sizes but different shapes. Invite students to take turns holding up their two rocks and indicating the one that they think is bigger. Then have students suggest ways to get more exact information about which rock is actually bigger. Ask students to listen while you read the following story aloud:

Archimedes' Story

Long ago, in a country called Greece, the king had a crown made for himself. It was a fancy gold crown, and the king was very pleased with it. Pleased, that is, until he began to notice that it just didn't shine like his other gold things. He began to wonder if it was made of solid gold, or if the person who had made the crown had mixed the gold with something else. The crown maker could then have kept the leftover gold for himself and cheated the king! The more the king thought about this, the more upset he got. He could melt the crown down to see if it were all gold, but then his crown would be ruined. He needed a better way to check. He decided to ask a scientist and inventor named Archimedes to work on the problem.

Archimedes thought and thought. If he knew how much gold the crown should have taken, he could take a piece of gold that was that big and weigh it. Gold is very heavy, and if there was another metal replacing some of the gold, the crown would not weigh as much as the same amount of pure gold. But how much gold should be in the crown? It was such a fancy shape with little gold lions and long points and fancy curves.

Archimedes was still thinking about the problem when he got undressed to take his bath. Then he sat down in the tub, and what do you think he noticed? The level of the water went up! The water had moved over to the side to make room for Archimedes. When he stood up, the water level dropped. When he sat down, the water level went back up to the same place it had been before. Archimedes was thrilled. He jumped from the tub and ran to tell the king he had solved the problem. He ran through the streets yelling "Eureka!," which means, "I found it!" The only problem is that in all the excitement he forgot to put his clothes back on!

You can review the story in the following way: *What was Archimedes' solution?* He took the king's crown, put it into a tub of water, and measured how much the water went up. Next, he took the crown out and put little pieces of gold in until the water went up just as high. Then he weighed the crown and all the gold. The gold was heavier. That meant the crown maker had cheated the king. Part of the gold had been replaced with a cheaper metal.

Ask: *How could you use Archimedes' discovery to find out which of your two rocks is bigger?* After students have answered, have each student choose that one of their two rocks which they expect would push more water aside if it were dropped into water.

Working in small groups, have students each fill a clear plastic glass halfway up with water and attach a strip of masking tape from the top to the bottom of the glass. Each student should then drop one rock into the glass and make a mark either with a pencil or marker on the tape at the new water level. Have the student remove the rock before repeating this process with the other rock. Have group members compare their results.

Call students together for a discussion. Ask: *Did the water go up the same amount every time a rock was placed in the water? What did happen? What did all the different results tell you?*

Investigating Structure with a Magnifying Glass Some rocks, such as quartz, granite, and sandstone, and several minerals, like pyrite, have crystal structures which can easily be seen with a magnifying glass. Introduce students to crystal structures by having them look closely at rock candy. Have students talk about what they see—shapes, flat surfaces, and sharp corners. Next, distribute magnifying glasses, and allow students to examine them briefly. Then ask students to look at salt and sand, first without and then through their magnifying glasses. Ask: *Do the magnifying glasses help you to see the same kinds of shapes in the salt and sand that you just saw with the rock candy? Do you think you will find any of these crystal shapes on any of your rocks? Why, or why not?*

Working in small groups, have each student sort his or her rocks into two piles, those that are likely to have crystal shapes, and those that aren't. Then have students use magnifying glasses to look for crystals. Encourage students to describe to each other in detail what they are seeing. Ask: *Which rocks have crystals, and which ones don't? Which have crystals all over, and which have them only in some places?*

FURTHER EXPLORATION

Students can work with you or another adult to make their own rock candy. Dissolve a substantial amount of sugar in hot water and pour the solution into jars. Attach strings to pencils and arrange them so a string hangs in the solution in each jar. If you use a clean paper clip to weigh down the end of each string, it will hang straight down. Allow a week for crystals to grow.

The Hardness Experiment

OVERVIEW

In this activity, students will test the relative hardness of different rocks by scratching them with known rocks. A scratch test is a common field test used by geologists to identify unknown rocks by scratching them with known rocks.

MATERIALS

- a variety of rocks of differing hardness (from students' rock collections)
- magnifying glass (optional)

ACTIVITY

Students begin by discussing what they have already done with their rocks and what they learned as a result. Next, ask students to predict which of their rocks will be the hardest. *Big rocks? Heavy rocks? Rocks with crystals? Rocks without crystals?* Students can make their predictions by arranging their rocks on a paper from hardest to softest. Suggest that students label their rocks with letters on tape, so they will later be able to compare their predictions with the results of the experiment they are about to do.

Explain that scientists who study rocks are called geologists. Geologists developed what is known as a scratch test to help to identify different kinds of rocks. A scratch test works by using one rock to try and scratch another. If two rocks are able to scratch each other slightly, they are probably of similar hardness, and they should be grouped together as the same kind of rocks. So geologists keep scratching an unknown rock with known rocks until they notice a slight scratch.

Let students take two rocks and try to scratch one rock with another. Then ask students to wipe the scratch with a finger to wipe off any "rock dust". This will determine whether there is an actual dent in the scratched rock. Point out to students that a magnifying glass can also help them to see the results of their scratch test. Tell students that if the unknown rock is softer than the known rock, the scratch on the unknown rock will be deeper; if the unknown rock is harder than the known rock, there may be no scratch at all.

Students can now go ahead and perform scratch tests on some of their rocks to establish an order of hardness. Students can then arrange their rocks in that order. You might suggest that they display only one rock of each kind.

Ask students to compare the results of their scratch tests with their predictions. Many students will not have predicted the order that the scratch test will show. If time allows, each student can display and describe the hardest rock from his or her collection. Since certain hard rocks, such as quartz or granite, have crystals which can be seen through a magnifying glass, students might also examine the hardest rocks to see if they contain crystals. They could then make guesses as to how the crystals may have helped the rocks be stronger.

FURTHER EXPLORATION

Students can follow up the activities in this unit by making up their own experiments with their rocks. They can also glue their rocks onto posterboard and label some of them as "hardest," "biggest," "crystals," "no crystals," and so on. Students may enjoy taking their collections home or showing them to other classes.

UNIT 2

Forces Around Us

The activities in this unit are designed to make students aware of forces and how they are a part of our everyday lives. Forces are the most basic element in the study of physics and chemistry, and an integral part of biology. Forces make things move and make things stop. Forces crush and deform. Forces help us to move, yet, at the same time, they limit our movement.

The activities in this section build on one another. The first activity serves to define the term force as a push or pull, and links force to motion. This definition of force is an integral part of all of the activities that follow. The second activity introduces the concept of friction as a force that opposes motion, slowing two objects down when they rub against each other. The concept of friction plays a role in the third activity, in which students experiment with the forces of gravity. In the fourth activity, students observe the cause and effect relationship between force and motion. The fifth activity deals with changing the direction of a force by using a pulley.

While it is possible to do these activities in any order, it is strongly suggested that they be done in sequence to maximize their benifit to the students.

What Is a Force?

OVERVIEW

This activity introduces students to the concept of force and its relation to motion. A force is a push or a pull. While forces affect everything around us, the source of the push or pull is often hidden. Think of a wind-up toy that looks like a dinosaur. The basic mechanism that makes the toy go is completely hidden, so it is impossible to see the internal spring that pushes on gears to make things move. In this activity, however, the mechanism that causes movement is simple and obvious. An elastic loop is hooked under the legs of chairs or tables, and students take turns using the elastic to shoot blocks across the floor.

Students are encouraged to make the connection between how far they pull the elastic back and the distance the block travels. How far back a student pulls the elastic is a measure of the push the elastic will exert on the block. The greater the force, the greater the distance that a block will travel. Doubling up on the elastic or using wider elastic will make the shooter even stronger, so it will take less of a pull to get the block to go the same distance. Students will tell you that it takes more effort to pull the wider elastic back than to pull a thinner one. This is because it takes a given amount of energy to get a block to travel a set distance. That energy can be released either with a weaker elastic and a long pull or a stiff elastic, a shorter pull, and more effort.

MATERIALS

Provide one shooter station for each small group of students. Each station will need:

- one two-foot piece of ½"-wide elastic (sold by the foot or in packages at fabric stores) with the ends sewn together to form a loop
- wooden blocks, about 4" x 2" x 1"
- one heavy table, one desk, or two chairs to provide two legs around which to loop the elastic
- masking tape
- string
- rulers and yardsticks (optional)

ACTIVITY

First, loop the elastic either under one leg of two chairs or around two legs of the table or desk, so that it is stretched out taut, nearly touching the ground. (When using chairs, have a student sitting on each one to weight it down.) This gives a double layer of elastic shooter. Have students stand safely behind the shooter. Then demonstrate how to place the block flat on the ground, pull it and the elastic back as far as possible, and then release them, shooting the block across the room.

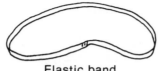

Elastic band

Block pulled back
against elastic

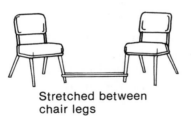

Stretched between
chair legs

And released

Next, under adult supervision, invite students to take turns experimenting with the elastic and blocks. Encourage them to try pulling the elastic back different amounts, placing the block on its different sides, or tightening the elastic by moving the table legs further apart. As students experiment, have them discuss what they observe.

When every student has had a turn, hold a class discussion about the activity. Ask such questions as: *What did you see happening? What seemed to change how far the block traveled?* Introduce the term force and define it as a push or pull on something. Then discuss when and how the block was pushed and pulled. A person first pulled back on the elastic. Then, when the person let go of the elastic, it pushed the block across the floor.

Ask the students what they would do with the elastic if they wanted the block to go a very long way or a very short way. Students' suggestions will probably include varying how far the elastic is pulled back. Help students generate a hypothesis such as the following: the farther the elastic is pulled back, the farther the block will go. Don't be concerned if the students think that the less the elastic is pulled back, the farther the block will go. Either of these is a hypothesis that can be tested. (If students offer other ideas, such as varying elastic tension, these, too, may work as hypotheses that can be tested.)

Have students work in small groups to test their hypotheses. Students should experiment by pulling their elastic back different amounts and marking the block's path. Instruct students to begin by choosing one person to pull the elastic back, while another student marks the starting point and then how far back it is pulled by putting masking tape on the floor in both places. Once the student releases the elastic, have another student mark with tape the block's final resting place. Have students then run a string through the three tapes, taping the string down to clearly mark the distance. Each time another student has a turn, the same procedure should be followed. Students, who have had experience with standard measurement, may wish to use rulers to measure the distances.

When all of the data points are recorded with string, the teacher can help students to interpret what they see. Young students may first need to review what each of the masking tape markers stood for and what the string shows. Students should see that the farther the elastic was pulled back, the farther the block traveled. Students should conclude that when the elastic was not pulled back very far, the block did not go very far, and when the elastic was pulled back far, the block went a long way. Finally, ask students to discuss these results and compare them to the hypothesis generated by the class.

FURTHER EXPLORATION

Encourage students to discuss other things they might want to test for. You might ask: *Does the size of the block make a difference in how far it will travel? What would happen if a ball was used instead of a block? What would happen if two elastic bands were used instead of one? What difference would a thicker or thinner elastic band make?*

If time permits, allow students to try their own experiments. You might prefer to transfer part of the activity to a learning center. There, a rubberband looped around two nails that have been hammered into a board can be used as the elastic shooter, and the items shot can be matchboxes.

Friction Is a Kind of Force

OVERVIEW

This activity introduces students to the concept of friction. Every surface has some roughness to it. Rubbing two surfaces together causes the roughnesses to "catch" a bit on each other, and generates a frictional force that opposes the motion. Friction is the combination of the two surface roughnesses and the pressure squashing them together. Students find that friction is the force that slows things down when two objects rub together. Increasing the weight of the sliding object increases the pressure squashing the surfaces together and increases the friction.

Students will run block races, in which they slide wooden blocks down the lanes of a track, each lane having been lined with a material of a different texture. Students are encouraged to classify the surfaces as rough or smooth; more experienced students can try to organize these sequentially. All students are asked to predict which block will be the first one down the track each time. This activity should take place over several days so that everyone can experiment fully.

Since friction exists between all surfaces, no system can ever be 100% efficient, because some of the energy will be lost. On the other hand, some friction is necessary; without friction, it would not be possible to have traction, and nothing could move.

MATERIALS

- one large cardboard box (the size of a moving company carton) or plywood, ¼ to ⅜" thick and 4' x 4' long
- duct tape
- continuous strips of burlap, sandpaper, foam sheet packing, plastic screening, carpeting, and various smooth materials (such as shopping bag paper, newspaper, bulletin board paper, fabric remnants)
- four to six wooden blocks, all the same size
- furring strips (such as dowel rods or thin strips of wood)
- pipe cleaners and popsicle sticks (if cardboard box is used)
- nails or screws (if plywood is used)
- heavy string or rope
- other objects to slide down the track (for example, blocks that differ from the standard racing blocks, items that can roll, blocks with sandpaper on one side)

PLANNING AHEAD

The main piece of equipment for this activity is a friction race track with four to six lanes for blocks to slide down. The friction track can be constructed of cardboard or the more durable plywood. If cardboard is being used, collapse a large cardboard box to give the track extra strength.

Tape the ends flat so that the box does not open up. The track should be about 4' square. If you use plywood, you will need half of a 4' x 8' sheet (¼ to ⅜" thick).

Line the separate lanes with continuous strips of various material. Try to avoid seams, and make sure that at least one material is smooth. Separate the lanes of the track with the furring strips you have obtained. Secure them to a cardboard track with pipecleaners and popsicle sticks, as shown, or to a wooden track with nails or screws.

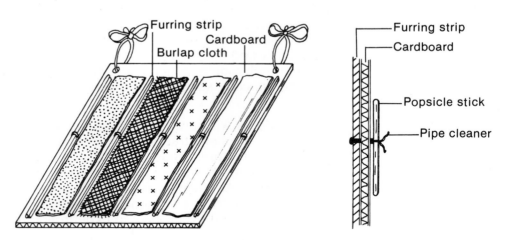

Set the track at an angle so that the blocks will slide down. To secure the track and be able to take it down easily, put one hole in each of the two upper corners of the track. Then put a rope through each hole. Tie the top of the track to a table turned on its side, or to any other piece of furniture that allows students to stand at the top of the track while other students sit around the base of the track, waiting their turn. When not in use, store the track flat against a wall.

ACTIVITY

Begin by giving students a few minutes to look at the friction track, feel it, and discuss what they observe. Next, place a block at the top of one lane and release it while students watch its descent. Then, as students continue to observe, place two or three similar blocks at the top of other lanes and release them simultaneously.

Now, explain to students that they will be having block races, and each student will be able to send a block down a lane on the track. Encourage students to discuss similarities and differences among the blocks and the lanes they will travel in. Then have students feel the lanes and select both the smoothest and the roughest. Have students predict down which track the winning block will go. Ask students to explain the thinking behind their predictions.

Now have students take turns racing their blocks. Caution students to simply let go of the blocks and not push them. Allow every student to run several races on several different lanes. After each race, students should announce the winning block, observing the type of track it was on. Have them record this information on a chart or graph to use in follow-up class discussions.

The first day that students engage in this activity, and on other occasions thereafter, bring everyone together for a discussion. Ask: *Did your guesses match your results? Which blocks won most often? Why?*

Students' observations can be expanded when they try their own experiments. These might involve such activities as sending blocks down on their sides, racing two blocks of different sizes, or taping a second block on top of the first to increase the mass. In these additional experiments, students are encouraged to explore; they do not need to find any particular relationship, although it is likely that they will begin to recognize some of the factors that contribute to friction.

FURTHER EXPLORATION

Together with students, name other objects that can be used on the track. To get things started, ask: *Which materials do you guess will go down the track the fastest, a smooth block or one with sandpaper on the bottom; a rectangular block or a sphere; a heavy block or a light one?* Provide students with the objects they will need to experiment. Then have students, working in small groups or in pairs, use the friction track to test their hypotheses.

Afterwards, review what students have observed about friction. Encourage students to share and discuss information from these experiments. Help students to consider how differences in results or conclusions might be tested.

Gravity Is a Kind of Force

OVERVIEW

This activity introduces students to the concept of gravity. Gravity is a force that is not well understood by the scientific world, yet it affects all of us. We know that there is gravity between any two objects, and that the amount of gravity depends on the mass of the objects. On the earth, the earth's mass pulls everything to it. The more the mass of both objects, (for example, the earth and a person), the greater the pull. Weight is a measure of the gravitational attraction between an object and the earth. That is why more massive people weigh more than smaller people.

In these activities, students first experiment by dropping items and observing that these items always fall down. Next, they roll toy cars down an inclined track that they adjust to various angles. Students observe that the steeper the incline, the farther the cars will travel across the floor after leaving the track.

In addition to gravity, this activity also explores the concept of conservation of energy: the energy used to raise any object is not lost, but is saved until the object is dropped. It requires energy for any object to move away from the earth and its gravity. If this object is then dropped, this energy is released in the form of motion. Thus, in this activity, the greater the height from which the toy car started moving, the more energy there will be at work in the system, and the farther the car will roll across the floor (assuming it is not stopped by another object). Because more massive objects have a greater gravitational pull, heavier cars will roll farther than lighter ones (everything else being equal). The energy stored is a function both of the height the car is raised and the car's mass.

MATERIALS

Provide two ramps for each small group. Each small group will need:

- two pieces of cardboard of equal length for the ramps (stiff enough not to sag under the weight of the cars)
- two identical small, easy-rolling toy cars
- four pieces of cardboard, about 8" by 1½", for the height adjustment stands
- masking tape
- duct tape
- paper clips (for the height adjustments stands)
- nails
- string
- scissors
- rulers and yardsticks (optional)
- clay (optional)

Note: This experiment works best on a smooth floor.

PLANNING AHEAD

Tape two nails on the back of each cardboard ramp as shown. To construct the height adjustment stand, follow the steps below.

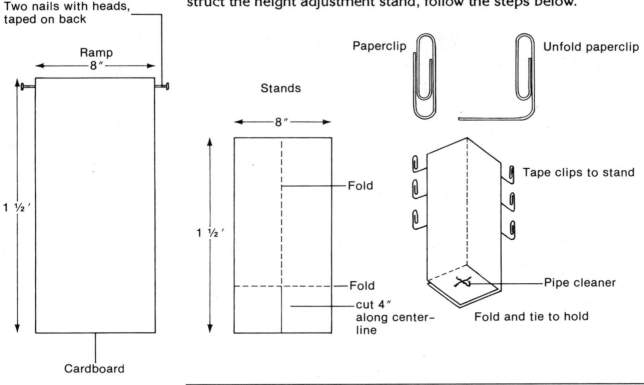

ACTIVITY

Begin by helping students tape the base of the ramps to the floor. Then show students how to adjust each of their two ramps at different angles by looping string around the ramp nails and then around the paper clips on the height adjustment stands.

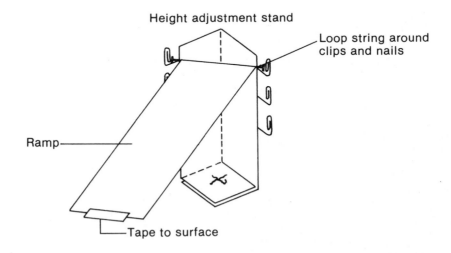

Explain to students that they will be using their ramps shortly. Ask students to first hold up and drop non-breakable objects such as their pencils and talk briefly about what happens. Then, have students jump up in the air once or twice and, again, tell what happens each time. Ask: *Why do you think the pencils fell down? Why do you think you didn't stay up in the air when you jumped?*

Next, have students, in groups, examine one of their ramps and predict what would happen if they placed a toy car at the top. Give students a moment to test their predictions with one of their cars. (Make sure, throughout this activity, that students simply let go of the cars at the top of the track and do not give the cars a push.)

After the students have had a chance to observe their car rolling down a track, stop the activity to discuss their observations. Ask: *What is making the cars roll down the track?* Then, define the term gravity: *Gravity is a force that pulls the cars toward the ground.*

Next, have each group look at the two ramps and say what is the same and what is different about them. (The only difference should be their angle of incline.) Have students let go of one car at the top of each ramp and observe what happens.

Ask students to guess which of their two tracks will take a car farther. Help them to generate hypotheses. Then ask how students could test to see if their hypotheses are correct.

Now have students experiment with different ramps, arranged at different angles. You may find it useful to assign two students to start the cars, one to do a countdown, and one to put down the tape marker. Because starting the cars may be the most popular job, it might be wise to have students switch roles occasionally.

As students experiment, have them observe and discuss the distance each car goes in relation to the angle of the ramp. Students can determine which car went farthest by looking at the pieces of tape marking the stopping point of each car. Students with experience in standard measurement may wish to use rulers to measure the distances.

When students have had ample time for this activity, hold a class discussion, during which they share and consider their findings. You might want to focus the discussion, by asking: *What seems to make a difference in how far a car will go after leaving the track? Did the car on the steeper ramp always go farther? Why, or why not?*

FURTHER EXPLORATION

Invite students to suggest other ramp experiments. Some ideas are: using the friction track from Lesson 2 at different angles; using balls, marbles, or wooden blocks instead of cars. Students might also want to use clay to add weight to their cars.

Leave the ramps up for several days so that students can bring objects from home to test. Encourage students to be on the lookout for inclines outside of school. Ask such questions as: *Why do many building entrances have ramps outside of them as well as stairs? How steep should the ramps be? What happens if you ride your tricycle or bicycle down a steep driveway? Which slide on the playground would you expect to be the fastest, a steep one or a flat one? Does the height of the slide always determine the speed?*

Forces and Motion

OVERVIEW

As you already know, force is a push or a pull. It is made up of two elements: magnitude and direction. Magnitude refers to the strength of the push or pull, and direction refers to the direction of the push or pull.

In the real world, many forces act on objects around us. For example, a block sitting on the sidewalk might have several forces acting on it: gravity pulls the block down into the sidewalk while the inter-molecular forces in the sidewalk push back with an equal force. If a slight breeze were blowing on the block, then a small amount of friction would push back. Here, two pairs of forces are at work. One is gravity and the sidewalk; the other is the wind and friction. Since the block is not moving, the forces are all balanced, so they cancel each other out. If the forces become unbalanced, the block would start to move.

In this activity, students experiment with force and motion by pushing blocks, dropping blocks, and hitting one block with another. Each time, students try to identify both where the force is coming from and in what direction the block will move. The movement of the block will always be in the direction that the force was applied.

MATERIALS

- wooden blocks (at least two per student or pair of students)
- string
- paper dots or washable magic marker

ACTIVITY

Begin the lesson by reviewing with students the concept of force. Then have students suggest ways they might apply force to move their blocks. After discussing safe and unsafe ways to move the blocks, let students try out some of their suggestions.

Then have students continue experimenting with applying force to their blocks. Some of the things they can try would be to push on their blocks using only one finger, push one block with another, and drop a block onto the floor.

At this point, stop the activity for feedback and discussion. Ask: *What happened when you pushed your blocks? What happened when you dropped them? Where do you think the force came from when you pushed the block? When you dropped the blocks, what force do you think was acting?* If necessary, help students to realize that their own strength, or muscle force, pushed the blocks; but when the blocks fell, it was the force of gravity that was operating.

Now ask: *Since a force is a push or a pull, if you pulled on a block, would it move in the same direction it moved when you pushed it?*

Students can test their hypotheses by taping a string onto the blocks, pulling the blocks toward themselves, then pushing them away with a finger, and comparing the results.

Next, say: *You have seen that when you push a block, it moves away from you, and when you pull it, it moves toward you. Do you think you can tell exactly what direction it will move every time you push or pull it?*

Have students experiment with pushing and pulling by using both a block with string and a block on which a visible dot has been placed directly in the center. For the pushing activity, students should first put one finger on the dot and push the block. (The block should move straight in the direction of the force.) Then students can place a finger slightly to the side of the dot and push. (The block will tend to spin as it moves.) Before each push, have students predict which way the block will move. Encourage students to discuss what is happening as they work. Next, have students conduct a similar pulling experiment. Again, students should make predictions about the direction in which blocks will move when pulled one way and then another.

When you think students have worked long enough with the blocks, call everyone together. Students can compare their results and draw conclusions.

FURTHER EXPLORATION

Students can investigate what happens when a block gets more than one force. (It moves in a direction which is the net result of the forces.) For this activity, students can use a very large cardboard box. Working on a smooth surface, such as linoleum floor, have one student slowly push the box. Stop and talk about in which direction it moved. Then have two students push on the box from different, but not opposite, directions. Now, add another student, and have them do the same thing. Finally, have two students position themselves opposite each other, and push the box. After the pushing, discuss with students what they observed. Encourage students to speculate about cause and effect relationships. (When opposite and equal forces push against each other, they cancel each other out.)

Changing the Direction of the Force

OVERVIEW

Pulleys are used to change the direction of a force and give mechanical advantage. One of the earlier inventions, pulleys continue to be very useful in the world today. You can see pulleys everywhere, from large construction cranes to the drill at the dentist's office.

Pulleys are composed of a wheel, which is grooved to keep a rope on track, a bracket that holds the wheel while allowing it to turn, and some device for anchoring the pulley bracket. As the rope is pulled, the wheel turns, allowing the rope to move in a changed direction with very little friction.

In this activity, students will identify a pulley, examine its parts, and understand their function. They will also discover how the pulley works to change the direction of a force. They will observe that, by pulling the string from the pulley down, they cause the string to move, which has the effect of lifting the weight. This cause and effect sequence is the most important concept for students to grasp.

They will also have the opportunity to use more than one pulley to discover that the force needed to pull an object decreases as the number of pulleys used increases.

MATERIALS

For each group of students, you will need:

- one pulley (a 1" diameter wheel is large enough)
- four to five feet of string (cotton cord)
- one truck or other small toy weighing about one pound, with a loop of string attached
- three or four other objects of different weights

Note: Pulleys can be tied by their mounting bracket to the handle of a file cabinet or a desk drawer, a hook on a chalkboard, or to any horizontal rod.

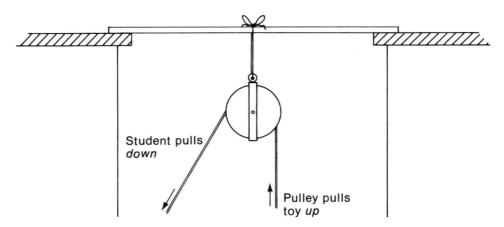

Student pulls *down*

Pulley pulls toy *up*

ACTIVITY

Begin by allowing the students to examine and handle the pulleys before they are mounted. Discuss the components of the pulley: the wheel; the bracket; the groove in the wheel; and the string. Encourage students to talk about how the wheel moves and what then happens to the string.

Next, mount the pulleys. Then ask students how they might use the pulley and string to lift the truck (or other toy). Students might just want to tie the string onto the truck and ignore the pulley; but encourage them to use the string that runs through the pulley. Give students time to experiment and discover. Have students consider the following questions as they work: *In what direction does the truck move when you pull the string? Does the truck always go up when the string goes down? What happens when the string goes up again? What if you pull the string out the left or the right instead of straight down?*

Now have students try lifting other objects of different weights and consider the same questions.

Conclude the activity with a discussion. Ask: *What does each part of the pulley do? What does the entire pulley do? When would a pulley be useful? What are some pulleys you have seen?*

FURTHER EXPLORATION

Students can add another pulley to the system and answer for themselves such questions as: *When two pulleys are used, will the direction the string is pulled be the opposite of the direction that the object is lifted? Will the force needed to lift the object be the same as when only one pulley is used?* If you wish, students can use a hand-held spring scale to determine the amount of force needed. After students are done working, ask: *When would it be useful to use more than one pulley? What would be the effect of using a third or fourth pulley?*

UNIT 3

Motion

The natural result of a force is a motion. Sir Isaac Newton was the first to define the relationship between force and motion. He asserted that an unbalanced force makes things move. According to Newton, forces both set things into motion, and forces stop motion. Forces make things move faster, and forces change the direction of the motion. (The larger the force, the greater the movement.) Newton said that force is equal to the mass of an object multiplied by its acceleration ($F = ma$).

The activities in this unit help students to explore the relationship between force and motion. Students are given opportunities to identify forces and the resulting motion in a variety of situations. This allows students to see how the cause and effect nature of the relationship between force and motion affects the world around us.

In the first activity, students observe the cause and effect relationship between force and motion by releasing balloon rockets and observing how they behave. The second activity deals with a pendulum and simple harmonic motion. Here, students focus on what causes the pendulum's motion. The third activity continues the investigation of friction, and allows students to actively experience the force and direction of friction. Both by moving things and by being moved, students observe that friction consistently opposes motion. In the fourth activity, students experiment with the direction and speed of various pulley arrangements. The last activity in this unit is about collisions. Students work with balls, making them collide into a barrier and observing the relationship between the angle at which each ball hits and the angle at which it bounces off the barrier. Students also measure the bounciness of various balls.

Forces That We Control

OVERVIEW

Aerospace engineering and space exploration occupy a special place of interest and excitement in everyone's mind. There is the thrill of the unknown, the glamour of the space program, and the wonder of human ingenuity. In this activity, students use balloons to make simplified model rockets. These rockets simulate one of the most exciting parts of space travel—the launch.

Students' balloons are confined to a string track by a drinking-straw guide. After balloons are launched, students keep track of such factors as the diameter of the balloon, the material the track is made of, and its slope. They make hypotheses about which elements will affect the distance their balloon travels, and then test out their guesses, and discuss the results.

When a rocket lifts off the launch pad, the solid and liquid fuel rockets are pushing out onto the air with tremendous force. This, in turn, pushes the rocket up into space. How far up the rocket will go depends on several factors, including how much fuel is on board, how fast the fuel is burned, and how massive, or heavy, the rocket is. For every action, there is an equal and opposite reaction.

Young students can't be expected to understand this technical explanation. However, they can come to realize that there is a cause and effect relationship between air escaping a balloon and the upward thrust of the balloon.

MATERIALS

For each group of students:

- at least three or four balloons of different sizes and shapes
- one piece of string or one piece of fishing line each at least nine feet long to be tied taut to two objects in the classroom, or to be tied to an object on one end and held taut by a student on the other end
- a plastic drinking straw, cut in 1 to 3" pieces
- duct tape

PLANNING AHEAD

If you wish to set up the experiment beforehand, cut and tie up string tracks, pulling the string relatively tight between points, and being sure to thread on a piece of drinking straw before tying the second end. (This need not be done ahead of time, because it is relatively quick to do.) The strings should be horizontal in order that the rocket balloon stay on the track at the place where it runs out of air.

ACTIVITY

Invite students to talk about rocket launches by asking: *Have you ever seen a rocket take off into space? What do you see as a rocket goes up into the air?* Then tell students that they will be sending up balloon rockets. Next, blow up a balloon and let each student feel the air rush out of the neck as you slowly relax your fingers. Repeat this; this time, let go of the balloon, asking students to notice what happens to it.

Now, have students predict what will happen when you launch a balloon on the track. Then blow up a balloon and attach it to the straw on one of the tracks with duct tape, while one student squeezes the end of the balloon so no air escapes. Be sure the neck of the balloon is at the end of the track, so it can work as a nozzle and push the balloon down the track.

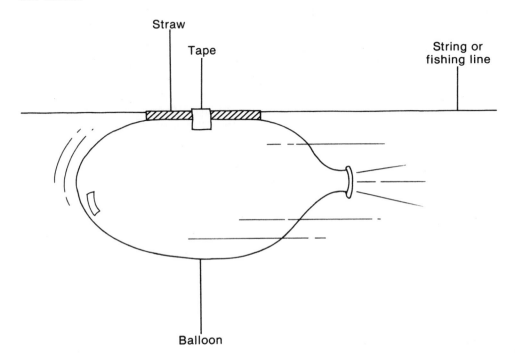

With students, count backwards from five to one, shout "Blast-off," and tell the student to release the balloon. Be sure students all have a clear view of what the balloon does. Then, try this again, this time using less air in the balloon. After each time, have students talk about what they saw happening. Now encourage students to experiment on their own tracks. Give each group time to try at least three or four launches.

Finally, call students together to discuss what they observed. You might guide the discussion by asking: *What did you see? Can anyone explain what made the balloon move?* If necessary, remind students of the air that came out of the neck of the balloon earlier. Ask: *What is pushing the rocket up the string?* Allow students ample time to observe and consider before guiding them to the conclusion that the air coming out of the balloon pushed on the surrounding air, and it, in turn, pushed back.

Ask the students what they might do if they wanted a balloon to travel farther away. Among the suggestions might be using a different string, making the string go downhill, and using a larger balloon. The simplest of these experiments would probably be varying the amount of air in the same balloon and testing the effect. You might want to run two tracks side-by-side with two different balloons so that the students can observe which has gone farther by simply looking at the end result. If you try this, be sure to have a great difference in the amount of air in the two balloons, keeping all other factors as similar as possible.

Before students experiment, have them make a prediction about what will happen and explain their thinking. After students have experimented, ask: *Did the balloons act the way you expected? What happened? Why do you think these things happened?*

Students might also experiment with balloons of various sizes and shapes. Afterwards, have students discuss such questions as: *Did the shape of the balloon have any effect on how far the balloons went? Did the size of the balloon matter?*

FURTHER EXPLORATION

Students who have gotten some understanding of the concept of gravity might investigate what happens if the track for the balloon rocket goes straight up. When they have sent two or three balloons up, ask them: *Why does the rocket go up and then come back down?*

Encourage students to come up with other experiments of their own. Leave the tracks up for several days so that students can test their hypotheses. Have students record their experiments and results either in words or with pictures.

This might be a good time to bring in simple books about flight to share with the students. Students may enjoy reading or hearing about the problems that early flight engineers faced.

Energy and Motion

OVERVIEW

In this activity, students will examine the swing of a pendulum and experiment with the factors that govern its motion. Kinetic energy is the energy of motion. This energy takes a swinging pendulum past the bottom and up again until gravity pulls it back down and the whole process repeats itself.

When a pendulum hangs straight down and is not moving, it is at its lowest energy state, and there it tends to remain. If a force is applied that moves it from its resting position, the pendulum tries to return to it, overshooting for a while until friction removes sufficient energy and the system comes to rest at the bottom of its swing. This kind of back and forth motion is called simple harmonic motion. However, if the motion were truly simple, there would be no friction, and the motion would go on forever.

Galileo was the first person to notice that as a pendulum's swing loses altitude, it also slows down. As a result, it takes just as long for the first swing as for one in the middle and one toward the end. This uniformity of motion became the basis for the first accurate mechanical clocks, in which a pendulum swung at the base of the clock and a weight slowly lowered, releasing its energy to the swinging pendulum. Because there was friction in the system, eventually the clock had to be wound to raise the weight again.

Two factors affect the swing of the pendulum. One variable is the length of the string, which has a very strong effect on the frequency of the swing: the longer the string, the fewer the swings per minute. Another variable is the height at which the pendulum is released: the higher the drop, the longer the distance traveled on each swing. The height generally does not affect the frequency.

MATERIALS

- a large clock with a second hand, visible to all students

For each individual pendulum:

- a metal washer
- heavy duty thread or string, cut to varying lengths

For classroom demonstration:

- one bowl, preferably clear
- one marble

PLANNING AHEAD

Depending on your students, you can either make pendulums in advance, or have students make their own. Make each pendulum by tying the washer onto the end of the thread or string. Older students can gain additional skill in measurement if they are asked to measure out the string before cutting.

ACTIVITY

Begin by having students experiment with their pendulums by changing the length of the string and the height at which they release the washer. Students should look for patterns as they observe what is happening.

After students have had sufficient time to try several changes, stop the activity for feedback and discussion. Ask: *What happened when the length of the string was changed? What happened when the height from which you let go of the washer was changed?*

Continue by asking: *If the length of the string is not changed, but the height at which you let the washer go is changed, will there be a different number of swings in ten seconds?* Allow time for guesses and discussion.

Have students test this questions by varying the height at which their washer is released and counting the number of swings in ten seconds. Encourage students to take turns counting the swings and watching the clock. Have them record their results. (You may want younger students to count the swings while an adult watches the clock.) Although some variation due to counting and clock-watching is inevitable, the number of swings in ten seconds should not change. Caution students to keep the length of the string the same as they change the height. After students have finished experimenting, you may want to write their results on the chalkboard.

Next ask students: *What will happen if the length of the string changes, but the height from which the weight is released doesn't?* Again, have students make predictions, test their hypotheses, record and discuss their results.

Talk with students about what factors affected the time for a pendulum swing, and what factors didn't. Then ask: *Why does the pendulum not just stop at the bottom of the first swing? What makes it move and what stops it?* Depending on the interest and age level of the group, you many want to discuss the motion of the pendulum, how gravity starts its fall, how energy carries it past the bottom of the swing and up the other side, and how gravity finally brings it to a stop, only to start the whole process over again. If so, use one of the pendulums to demonstrate the motion as you discuss it.

FURTHER EXPLORATION

Students can investigate whether the duration of the pendulum swing is independent of the weight of the washer. Have them tie three washers onto the same string and then time the swings. Suggest that they compare what happens to what happened with one washer swing. (The number of swings remains the same.)

Friction and Motion

OVERVIEW

In Unit Two, students learned that friction occurs when two things rub together, and that the rougher the two things are, the greater the friction. Friction is always with us, trying to slow down motion. We fight friction by using more energy to keep things going and by carefully designing things that move to have the least friction possible. In this activity, students try to discover specific causes of friction, and increase their understanding of the notion that friction is always opposing motion.

Although there are really two kinds of friction (dynamic and static), students will explore only dynamic friction. Dynamic friction is friction of an object in motion. Static friction is friction when something is stopped. Static friction normally is greater than dynamic friction. For that reason, when you push on a very heavy box, it is hard to get it to move, but once moving, it is much easier to keep the box moving than to let it stop and then have to start it from a resting position again.

This activity gives students an opportunity to be very physically active, and is best done in a gym, cafeteria, or playground. The study of friction and motion lends itself well to a day when students have extra energy they need to burn off.

MATERIALS

For a playground experiment:
- a slide
- a wagon
- a kickball
- a large sheet of cardboard, a rope, and tape or a wooden sled (optional)

For an indoor experiment:
- old socks
- pull toys
- a jump rope or other strong long rope
- large cardboard boxes, sticks or blocks, and rope
- tumbling or exercise mats

PLANNING AHEAD

If you are using playground equipment, it is probably already set up. If you decide to use a cardboard sled, put two holes in the cardboard, reinforce them with tape, and tie the rope to the cardboard. To make a cardboard box vehicle, punch a hole in the base of a box, slide a rope through the hole, and tie it around a stick or large block to keep it from pulling back out.

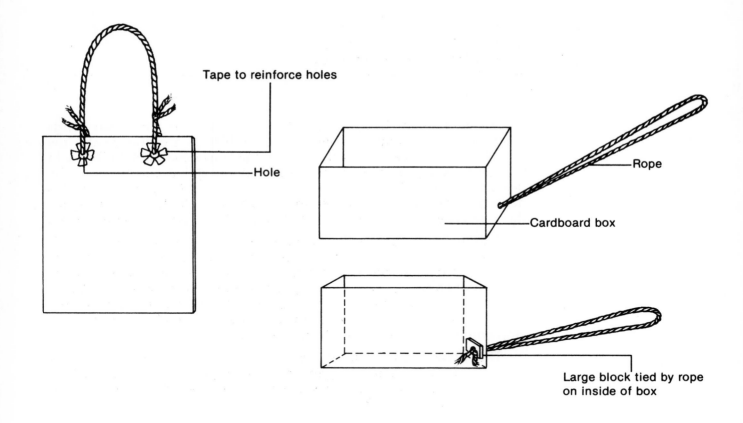

Tape to reinforce holes

Hole

Rope

Cardboard box

Large block tied by rope on inside of box

ACTIVITY

Talk about or demonstrate each piece of equipment you will be using for this activity. Tell the students that as they experiment with the materials, they should think about friction and how it is affecting motion. Then suggest that when students pull objects, they notice when they have to pull harder, and think about why this is so. If they use a kickball, they should observe how it behaves after it hits the ground. Ask students to try all of the activities. If students are experimenting outside, encourage them to pull their cardboard sled on dirt or grass, since pavement will quickly rip the cardboard. Unless there is snow on the ground, a real sled should also be kept off paved surfaces. Students can pull a wagon on hard dirt or grass, and then on a paved surface.

Inside, have students try to skate or slide on the floor with their old socks on, then try the same thing with their shoes on. Students can also pull tumbling mats across the floor and pull each other in cardboard boxes. Each time, students should notice when their movement was harder and when it was easier.

After everyone has tried the various activities, call students together for feedback and discussion. Ask: *What did you notice was rubbing as you [skated, slid, and so on]? At what time was it hard to move?*

The first time friction is identified, remind students that friction is a force and, as such, pushes. Then, each time friction is recognized, ask: *Which way was the friction pushing? Was it in the direction of the motion? Was it in the opposite direction?* Point out that if friction was pushing the way students were moving, they would speed up. If the friction was pushing in the opposite direction, it would tend to slow students down.

Now, have each student choose one favorite activity. Let students try the activity, moving in several directions. Have them think about whether friction ever speeds up their motion.

Finally, have students gather together for another discussion. Ask several volunteers what they did and whether friction speeded them up or slowed them down. Invite the rest of the students to give their opinions about how friction was acting. If there is a disagreement, allow students to do the particular activity again, then come together to discuss their conclusions.

FURTHER EXPLORATION

Sometimes, to reduce friction, we oil moving machine parts, use air under an air hockey game, and use bearings instead of rubbing parts. The reduction in friction this causes can be tested easily with bearings. (Students can see bearings on skate board wheels. Often, used bearings can be picked up at an automobile repair shop.) Bearings use round balls or cylindrical rollers. To demonstrate how bearings work, place a flat board (about 1' x 1') on an uncarpeted floor. First, have students try to push the board across the floor and discuss how it felt as it moved. Then lift the board up, put marbles on the floor, and place the board on the marbles. Students will observe that it now moves very freely. Have them talk about why this happens.

Pulleys, Direction, and Speed

OVERVIEW

Gears and pulleys are very closely related. Both are frequently used to change the speed and direction of a force. There are pulleys and belts on the front of your car's engine (your fan belt, for instance), on moveable clothes lines, in your sewing machine, and in your record player. Gears in your car's transmission control how fast your tires turn. There are also gears in music boxes, in wind-up toys, in electric mixers, mechanical clocks, and can openers. In fact, almost anything that moves with a motor has either a pulley or a gear system to make it work.

MATERIALS

For each group of students:

- one small wooden board
- nails
- empty spools of thread
- rubberbands

PLANNING AHEAD

Before the activity begins, prepare boards by hammering in nails to hold the empty spools. These will serve as pulleys.

ACTIVITY

As students watch, wrap rubberbands around every two pulleys. Ask students to notice what happens to one spool as you turn another. Then allow students to experiment themselves, first with two spools, and then with more than one pulley system. Suggest that students may want a rubberband to go around three pulleys, or have two rubberband set-ups, with one pulley in common. Students can try wrapping some of the rubberbands so that they cross. Direct students to observe how the motion is affected each time.

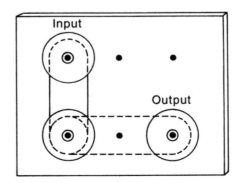

Next, have students make other pulley set-ups and predict the motion of the various pulleys. As an example, they may want to try a long pulley chain, with some rubberbands crossed and some not.

When students have experimented for some time, have them discuss their observations about kinds of pulleys and the resulting motion. You may wish to have students draw what they observe.

FURTHER EXPLORATION

Introduce a pulley with a small diameter on the same board (either a smaller spool, or one with the diameter filed down, or a bobbin). Have students predict whether a change in diameter will have any effect on the motion of the pulleys, and if so, what change. Then have students test their ideas. Ask them to check direction first. The smaller pulley will turn in the same direction as a large pulley. Then have students check speed by placing a pen dot on top of each pulley and turning the large pulley completely around two or three times. Ask students to observe how many times the small pulley went around. (The smaller pulley will turn around more times than the large pulley that is attached by the same rubberband.)

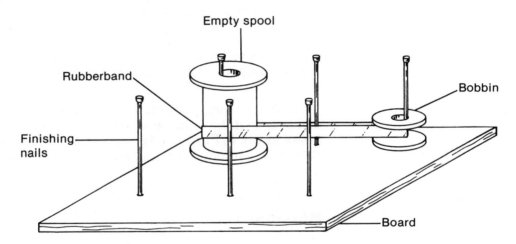

Collisions

OVERVIEW

This activity is designed to allow students to experiment with motion, mass, and collisions. A collision requires motion, that is, some object or mass has to move and collide with something else. In the simplest kind of collision, only one of the two colliding objects is in motion. When two objects collide, one of two things can happen: they can stick together or bounce apart. Bouncing apart, the most common outcome of the two, is the one students will experiment with here.

When objects hit and bounce, the direction in which they bounce is determined by the angle at which the two items collide. If a ball bounces against a wall and off again, the angle it leaves from is the same as the angle at which it hits.

As things collide, they deform. The amount of deformation depends on the amount of the mass and the energy involved in the collision. Sometimes things that collide deform and break. And sometimes they deform, store the energy just as energy is stored in a stretched spring, and then release that energy by returning rapidly to their original shape. This causes an object, such as a ball, to bounce back. Since some energy is lost to internal friction, no ball can bounce as high as the height from which it was dropped. The amount that it does bounce back is called its coefficient of restitution.

In this activity, students will roll golf balls against a board or a wall and discover that the angle at which the ball hits is also the angle at which it bounces off. In Further Exploration, students will also measure the coefficient of restitution, or bounciness of various balls.

MATERIALS

Each group will need:
- a golf ball
- several sheets of carbon paper
- several sheets of white 8½" x 11" paper
- a table (optional)
- masking tape
- a large piece of paper or posterboard (optional)
- five or six different types of round balls, from beach balls to ping pong balls (optional)

PLANNING AHEAD

Either place a table on its side, or use the wall as the object off which the golf ball will bounce. Using masking tape, mark a target spot on the table or the wall and mark several starting points about two feet from the barrier, as shown.

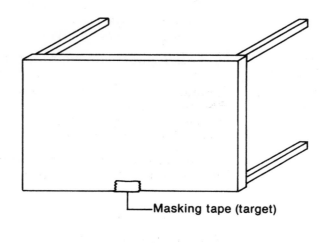

—Masking tape (target)

—Masking tape
(starting point)

Place carbon paper, carbon side down, over a white sheet of paper, and clip or staple the two sheets together. Then lay them snugly against the table or wall beneath the target spot.

ACTIVITY

To begin, explain to students that they will be rolling a golf ball from several different starting points toward the target spot, hard enough so that it will hit the table or wall and bounce off. As it rolls towards the barrier, it will leave a carbon track. The purpose of the experiment is to compare the paths of balls rolled from the different starting points. Tell students you will roll one ball to demonstrate what they will be doing. First, ask students what they think will happen when the ball hits the barrier. Ask: *What will it do? Where will it stop?* Once students have offered their predictions, stand at one marked point, and roll the golf ball. When it comes to a stop, have students examine the paper beneath the target point. Remove the carbon. Point out the path the ball made, as well as the incoming angle and the exiting angle. Next, fold the paper, as shown.

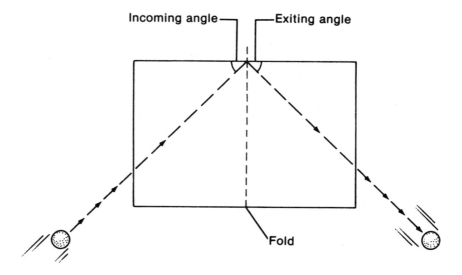

Incoming angle — — Exiting angle

Fold

Help the students to see that the two angles are the same. Ask: *What will happen if we roll the ball from different starting points? Will the ball always bounce back? Will the two angles always be the same?*

After students have made their predictions, allow them to experiment. Students can pair up and take turns placing the carbon and the white paper beneath the target and rolling the ball. Together they should examine the path, label the angles "in" and "out" respectively, and fold the paper to see if the angles are the same. Partners should roll the ball from several different starting points.

When students have completed their experiments, lead a discussion during which students can share their observations.

FURTHER EXPLORATION

In this activity, students can explore the bounciness of a ball. Stand the poster board against the wall or table and secure it with tape. Help students to draw horizontal lines every three inches along the posterboard. Then have various students, one at a time, release a different ball from above the posterboard while other students watch to see which line is closest to the height of the bounce. Just before dropping each ball, students should predict which balls will bounce higher. After each group of students has dropped several balls, groups should combine to share their findings about which balls bounced the highest and which bounced the least.

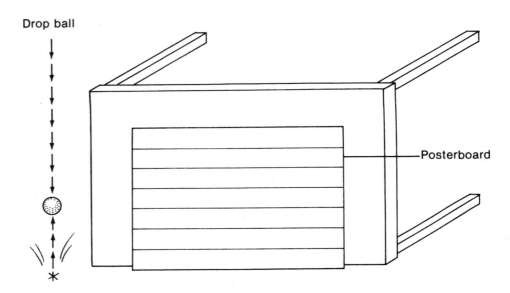

UNIT 4

Fluids In Motion

In this unit, the study of motion is expanded to include fluids. Students will explore some of the concepts they were introduced to earlier, as well as new concepts about motion that can be observed with liquids.

In the first activity, students investigate the behavior of waves by throwing objects into water and observing the results. Students also discover what happens when a wave hits an obstacle. In the second activity, students focus on the concept of viscosity and test the viscosity of various fluids. The third activity introduces students to the concept of evaporation. The last activity in this unit concerns erosion. Students discover that moving fluids can exert forces, even on very hard things. Students look at the effects of the erosion and consider preventive measures.

Waves

OVERVIEW

Sound, heat, light, and electricity all are carried by invisible waves. These waves are the basis for many unseen phenomena in our everyday lives. For example, radio waves send signals to our radios, TVs, and cordless phones, and light waves of different lengths determine the colors we perceive.

All waves move in a characteristic fashion. Therefore, before students try to grasp the concept of invisible waves, it is useful to allow them to experiment with waves they can see.

This activity is designed to provide an experience in which students investigate the creation of water waves. Students will make waves in water and observe the effects of actions, such as throwing a pebble in the water, using two pebbles, and putting a barrier in the water.

MATERIALS

For each station:

- large containers of various shapes (such as pots, buckets, pans, or a child's wading pool)
- pebbles
- a cookie sheet or other solid to use as an obstacle in the water

PLANNING AHEAD

Set up three or four stations for students, either outside or in a large indoor space. Place containers of different sizes and shapes in each station so that students can decide whether the size or shape of a container has any effect on the waves. If students are to work indoors, be sure to put a drop cloth under the water containers. You can also keep spills to a minimum by keeping water levels low, since only surface effects are important.

ACTIVITY

Let students explore freely for a few minutes by throwing pebbles into the water and watching what happens. Next, have students toss one pebble into different containers. Tell them to notice what happens, including the action that takes place at the edges of the container when the waves hit those edges.

After all the students have been able to observe the waves in at least two different containers, ask students to come together to discuss what they have observed. Ask: *Did you notice waves coming from the place where the pebble went into the water? What did the waves look like?*

What was their shape? Did the shape of each container change the shape of the wave? What happened when waves hit the edge of the container?

At this point, ask students to make two predictions: what will happen when they throw two pebbles into the water at the same time, and what will happen when waves run into some obstacle. After students have made their predictions, have them work in pairs to test their ideas. To experiment with two pebbles, one student can throw in the pebble, while the other student observes. Then they can switch roles and repeat the experiment. Each time, group members can draw a picture of the result. To investigate what happens when waves hit an obstacle, students can place either a cookie sheet or some other solid object into the water and repeat the process of dropping pebbles into the container.

When students have finished experimenting, hold a discussion during which they can talk about what they did and what they observed. You might ask: *When you throw two pebbles close together, what are the waves like? What happens when the waves reach each other? What happens to a wave after it hits an obstacle?*

FURTHER EXPLORATION

Students might continue the exploration of waves by looking at waves made in a jump rope. They can create waves by having one student hold the end of the jump rope still while another student whips the rope up and down. Tell students to observe and then describe the waves that are created. You might want to mention to students that the distance from the start to the end of one wave is called the wavelength, and the height is called the amplitude.

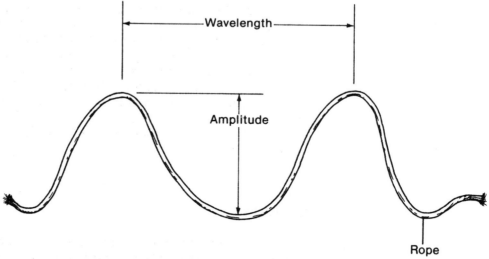

Ask: What happens to each wave in the rope when it reaches the end that is not moving? How does this compare to the wave from the pebble as it reaches the edge of the container?

Viscosity

OVERVIEW

Viscosity is the thickness of a fluid, and is determined by how easily the particles of a fluid move past each other.

Viscosity is a very important characteristic of a liquid. A liquid's viscosity determines how fast the liquid will pour. Viscosity is one of the main factors in determining whether a liquid will move smoothly as it flows, or if the flow will be turbulent.

Viscosity is one of the properties scientists use numbers to describe. They use what is called the coefficient of viscosity. In this activity, students won't actually determine the coefficient of viscosity, but they will test the viscosity of different liquids, then order them from the most to the least viscous.

Students may already be aware of the importance of viscosity without realizing it. For example, TV advertisements for syrup and catsup stress how thick their products are; thicker means more viscous.

MATERIALS

For each group of students:

- a paper cup
- a sharp pencil
- at least three different types of liquids (for example, edible liquids, such as water, corn syrup, vegetable oil, molasses, apple juice, prune juice, and evaporated milk; and inedible liquids, such as dishwashing soap, paint, shampoo, window cleaner, and bubble soap. (If the students are young, you may wish to avoid the inedible liquids for safety reasons.)
- a clock with a second hand, or a stopwatch (optional)
- small containers (such as the cut-off bottoms of two-liter soda bottles or gallon milk jugs, a large mixing bowl, or a dishpan)
- towels

ACTIVITY

First, explain to students that they are going to test the thickness of different fluids. Students should begin by putting a pencil mark about halfway up their cups. This will be the mark to which each liquid will be poured. Next, students can use a pencil to poke a hole about half a pencil-width wide in the bottom of the cup. (Experiment with this yourself beforehand to determine a good size for the hole.) The hole needs to be large enough so it won't take several minutes for molasses to pour out and small enough so you can actually time water before it all pours out. (Younger students may need help marking the fill line and poking a hole in the cup.)

Next, have students pour one of their liquids into their cups to the fill line while one student holds one finger over the hole in the bottom of the cup. When the cup is full, have that student hold the cup over the catching container; then ask the student to uncover the hole. Ask students to observe what happens to the liquid. Then have them try this with another liquid. Ask students what happened this time.

Continue by asking: *How could you tell which liquid poured out of the cup faster?* Have students pour another liquid and use a clock or stopwatch, or simple counting to time the liquid as it pours from the cup. Then have students record and report their results. Ask: *Why didn't both liquids take the same amount of time?*

Now, ask students to consider at least three liquids. Have them make a hypothesis about which will pour out of the cup the fastest and give a reason for their prediction. Then tell students to pour the liquids, one at a time, into the paper cup to the fill line while another student keeps a finger over the bottom hole. As the finger is removed, students time how long it takes for each liquid to pour into the container. Students can either record or remember the relative speeds.

After students have timed all their liquids, have them gather together to discuss the results. Ask: *Which liquid was the fastest of those you tested? Which was the slowest? What can you tell us about your other liquids? Was it the same for every group? Did the size of the hole make any difference?*

Tell students that the word that describes a liquid's thickness is viscous. Then ask students if they know which liquid is the most viscous. Establish that the slowest liquid will be the most viscous one. If it seems appropriate, explain that in the most viscous liquid, one part of the liquid slides slowly over another part. In other words, that liquid has a great deal of friction within itself.

FURTHER EXPLORATION

Students can observe whether temperature has any effect on the viscosity of a liquid. Corn syrup would be a good material for investigating this. Have students, working with an adult, put one bottle of corn syrup in the refrigerator, leave one at room temperature, and heat some gently in a pan on the stove. Ask students to predict whether the three syrups now have the same viscosity or thickness. Allow students, still working with an adult, to test each syrup using their paper cups. Have them record their results. Then ask: *What do you notice? Have you ever had trouble pouring cold syrup on pancakes? Why are these cold liquids so slow coming out of the bottle?*

Students can also test the viscosity of catsups. You might add some water to the cafeteria's catsup to ensure one very thin catsup.

Evaporation

OVERVIEW

Evaporation is the act of changing either a liquid or a solid into a gas or a vapor. This change is only physical, and doesn't change the chemical properties of the object. Matter is never created or destroyed (unless it is changed into energy according to Einstein's famous $E = mc^2$), but matter does change form, as when a liquid evaporates. For example, water remains H_2O, whether it is in the form of ice, a liquid, or steam. Evaporation fascinates children, who often wonder where the water has gone when they see a pot boil dry on the stove or puddles disappear on a sunny day. It may seem to them that magic has made the water disappear. This activity gives students a better understanding of what really happens to the water when it evaporates.

Students will begin the experiment by watching the steam that is given off from boiling water, then make a "human" model of water particles, and, finally, measure water before and after it has been heated to the boiling point.

MATERIALS

- a pan of water
- a small electric burner, a stove, or a steam vaporizer
- a sheet of black construction paper
- a flashlight (optional)
- masking tape, rope, or string
- a clear jar
- two clear measuring cups (optional)

ACTIVITY

Begin by asking students where water goes when a puddle dries. Then have students observe as you heat a pan of water to the boiling point. (Be careful to see that the students are a safe distance away.) Place a sheet of black construction paper behind the water so students can see the steam. Shining a flashlight on the steam will make the steam even more visible. Ask students if they recognize what they are seeing. Some students may think the steam is smoke. (You can demonstrate that water doesn't burn by dropping a lighted match into the water and watching it go out.)

Tell students that they are going to pretend to be the water in the pot. Ask them to stand in a circle, with each student holding onto the shoulders of the person in front. Before students continue, make a masking tape, string, or rope circle around them. Tell students that they are going to pretend to be tiny pieces of water that are always moving—both wiggling in place and moving in and out. Explain that as they get hotter, they will move faster and faster. Now have students experiment to see what happens when water is heated. Caution them to spread out a little if they are bumping onto each other. After a few seconds, tell students that the water is getting hotter. Remind them to move faster as they heat up. Do this three or four times, stopping each time to observe what happens.

Next, have students tell what happened as they began to move faster. Ask: *Did any of you—the little pieces of water—let go? Did the circle get bigger?* Then have the students predict what will happen as they pretend to heat up even more by moving around more quickly. Ask them to try it and see, being careful not to move too fast or to hurt anyone.

After students have moved around for a minute or so, ask: *Has the circle gotten bigger? How many pieces of water have let go now?* Explain that these are the particles of water that have evaporated, or left the pan and gone up into the air. Point out that if students continue the activity long enough, increasing their speed, everyone would eventually let go of each other and "evaporate." This is because, as water heats up, its molecules spread out and change into steam.

Have students tell what will happen if they measure the amount of the water in the pan before and after they heat it. Ask: *Will there be the same amount of water in the pan or will there be more, or less?*

Now, pour water into a clear jar, filling it to a line near the top. Mark that point on the jar. Then pour this water into the pan and heat it to the boiling point. Let it boil for a few minutes while you discuss with students what is happening. After the water has boiled for a while, remove the pan from the burner and let it cool down. Then pour the water back into the jar. Ask: *What point does the water come to now? Is it at the same level as before? Is there more or less water in the jar than when we began?* Have students discuss the result and how it compares to their predictions and then draw a picture of what happened. (Although younger students may have difficulty with the concept of conservation of liquids, they will be able to observe and make a comparison. Experienced students may be able to make comparisons using a measuring cup.)

FURTHER EXPLORATION

You may want to provide two clear measuring cups, which students can fill with water. They can leave one in a sunny spot in the classroom and the other in a cool, shady spot. Have students predict when each of the cups will be empty. Then every day, after lunch, have students note and record the number reached by the water in each of the cups. When both cups are empty, have students discuss what happened, and why.

Erosion

OVERVIEW

Both wind and water are responsible for much of what we call erosion. Moving water exerts forces that sometimes eat away at dirt and stone, carrying it off.

Moving water has a great deal of mass, and when it hits an object, that force can rip down buildings. But there is another factor in water erosion that increases its destructive power. As a river moves rapidly downstream, it erodes small pieces of rock, dirt, and other debris from the sides and bottom of its bed. These then act like the grit in sandpaper to further erode the sides of the bank downstream.

The problem with soil erosion is that most of the best dirt is on the top of the ground. For this reason, uncontrolled erosion can be very destructive to property, plants, and wildlife. Nature controls erosion very neatly by using the roots of plants to hold the soil in place. People place netting on the ground or logs on the sides of hills to slow down soil loss. Windbreaks of trees, a common sight in the Midwest, were created after erosion turned the heartland of America into the dustbowl during the Depression.

In this activity, students will experiment with water, observe its erosive effect on sand, and think of solutions to soil erosion.

MATERIALS

- a wading pool (if outdoors)
- plastic dishpan (if indoors)
- a bucket of sand
- a large bucket or two of water
- a cloth diaper or handkerchief
- small plastic soldiers or tiny plastic houses, trees, cars, and so on
- small pitchers, plastic two-cup measuring cups, or large plastic cups
- a sandbox shovel

ACTIVITY

Have students begin by building a damp mountain of sand in the wading pool or dishpan. (In a wading pool, tell students to put the sand off to one side so that they don't have to climb into the pool to get to the mountain.) Have students place some soldiers, cars, or other objects on the sand.

Next, have students take turns pouring water from their pitchers onto the sand mountain and observe what happens. It should be possible to see grooves forming in the mountain as the water carries off the sand, and a delta forming at the bottom as the water slows down and the sand settles out. As the groove grows, some of the soldiers and other objects will be undermined and washed away.

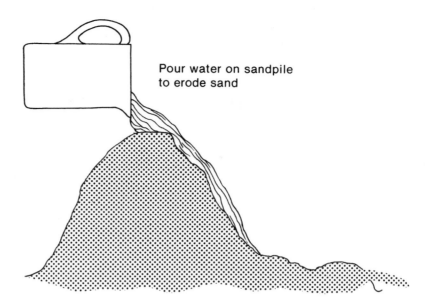

Pour water on sandpile
to erode sand

In a few minutes, stop the activity, gather everyone together near the pool or dishpan, and discuss what students are seeing. Either introduce or elicit the term erosion and talk about what erosion does to the land. Allow students to share their personal experience with erosion in action. Sometimes the effects of erosion can be beautiful, sometimes, messy.

Next, ask: *What would happen to the speed of the erosion if a diaper or handkerchief were placed on the side of the mountain?* Allow students to guess. Then have them place a diaper or handkerchief on the side of the sand mountain where the water is eroding. Two students can hold the top corners in place while other students pour water on the diaper or handkerchief. Invite observations. Students will probably notice that the erosion slows way down. Ask why. Point out that the cloth holds the sand in place just as the grass and tree roots hold the soil in place on a real mountain. Discuss how the cloth is like the plant roots. Ask: *In what other ways do people try to stop erosion?* Answers might include: by building dams; lining a river bed with concrete; and requiring replanting of strip-mined areas.

FURTHER EXPLORATION

At this point, students might experiment with other ways to stop the sand mountain from eroding. Among these might be using their hands to stop the flow and putting materials other than diapers and handkerchiefs in the sand. When they have finished experimenting, give students an opportunity to share their efforts. A walk around the schoolyard may reveal places where erosion has made grooves or dents, or washed large rocks clean. In addition, stories and pictures of the Grand Canyon, strip mining, or the Mississippi Delta can all enrich students' understanding of erosion. (Most large maps of the United States show the Mississippi Delta well enough so it can be easily identified.) During winter, in northern climates, snow that has been carved by wind can be easily seen from the classroom window.

Light

We see things because light bounces off objects into our eyes. Our eyes use light to give us information about the world. We gain information about where things are, what shape they have, what color they are, and how we expect them to feel just by looking at them.

In the first activity, students experiment with how information carried by light is understood by the viewer: as the amount of light goes down, the information, too, diminishes. Students are also able to see how eyes adjust to the amount of light available. In the second activity, students notice how light bounces off objects, just as a ball bounces off a wall, and they make observations about the relationship between the incoming light and outgoing light. The third activity involves rainbows and prisms, and allows students to see that light is made of many colors. In the fourth activity, students learn more about the connection between light and what they see by viewing their own puppet shows through transparent, translucent, and opaque screens.

Your Eyes and Light

OVERVIEW

In this activity, students investigate how their eyes use light to give them information about the world. The focus of the activity is on how the eye uses light information, rather than on the structure of the eye.

The eye uses light to form an image which the brain can interpret. In very low light, very little information is available and a fuzzy dark image is seen. As the light is increased, outlines and features become more distinct and colors and textures are more easily discerned.

MATERIAL

- multi-colored construction paper cut into squares (red, blue, brown, green, and purple)

ACTIVITY

Start by posing the following questions to the class: *How do you think your eyes get information about the world?* After a brief discussion, have students in pairs look at each other's eyes as you turn off all the lights. Ask: *What did you notice?* Students should be able to observe that the pupils of their partners' eyes responded to the change in light by enlarging. If they can't see each other's eyes, make the room slightly lighter. Now ask: *What was the only thing about the room that changed as your partner's eyes changed?* Students should realize that as the light diminished, the pupils enlarged. Their enlarged pupils allowed more light to enter their eyes.

Continue by giving students the squares of construction paper of five different colors. In an unlighted room (blinds drawn so the room is only dimly lit), have students try to sort the colored squares by placing a red square on one corner of their desk or table, a blue one on another, a brown one on a third, a green one on a fourth, and a purple one in the center. Ask: *What can you see on your desk?* Then, as you slowly raise or open the blinds, tell students to raise their hands when they can see the colors clearly. Now ask: *What was the only difference between the room with the blinds drawn and the room with them open? What can you say about light and color?* Help students to acknowledge that it took more light for them to see color than for them to see just general shapes.

FURTHER EXPLORATION

Students can extend the experiment by mixing up their construction paper squares and taking them to places with varying degree of light or darkness. Have students notice and remember those conditions in which it was impossible to discern color, and those that yielded enough light. Have students report their findings to the class.

Reflections

OVERVIEW

Light can travel as a particle or as a wave. In this activity, students will use mirrors to see how light travels as a particle. Students will experiment with a beam of light bouncing off a mirror. They should observe that when a thin beam of light hits a reflective surface, it bounces off, as a ball does. And like a rebounding ball, the light bounces off at the same angle it traveled when it hit. Put in scientific terms, the angle of incidence (or incoming angle) equals the angle of reflection (or outgoing angle).

Although students probably use mirrors everyday, they may not really understand how a mirror works. Mirrors are usually a piece of glass, coated on one side with a thin layer of a metal, such as aluminum. The metal provides a shiny surface and the glass keeps the metal from being damaged.

People see themselves in a mirror because light has hit their bodies, bounced into the mirror, bounced off the reflective back of the mirror, and then entered their eyes. In other words, a mirror works because the light that hits it bounces back off again.

The direction that light goes after it hits a mirror depends entirely on the direction it was going before it hit the mirror. In a normal room, there is light bouncing in many different directions. If the amount of light hitting the mirror is reduced to just a single beam of light, as in this experiment, the effect of the reflection will be much easier to see. The light beam will travel in a straight line, spreading somewhat as it travels (because not all of the light in the beam hits the mirror at the same angle). The light will be reflected, or bounced off the mirror, continuing to spread slowly. If a line is drawn down the center of this beam as it hits the mirror and as it bounces off, and the angle that each of these lines makes with the mirror is measured, the two angles will be found to be the same. (This is the same result that was found earlier when a golf ball was rolled across the floor, hit a barrier, and bounced off. In both cases, the angle of incidence was equal to the angle of reflection.)

In Further Exploration, students will build a simple kaleidoscope, which works by using more than one reflective surface to make many images of some pattern. Since each image is a copy or reversed copy of the original, the final result is symmetrical and, therefore, pleasing to the eye. Simple kaleidoscopes use two reflective surfaces. As with any multiple mirror system, there are more images than mirrors because the light bounces off more than one mirror before entering the viewer's eye.

MATERIALS

For each reflection station:

- one mirror
- a slide projector without a slide or a standard light bulb in a lamp
- a strip of posterboard with a thin slot cut out of one side

- tape
- scissors
- writing paper, pencil, hand mirrors (optional)

For each kaleidoscope (optional):

- two small pieces of cardboard, approximately 3" x 5" each
- aluminum foil or metalized plastic
- two mirrors (which can be taken from the reflection station)
- tape
- toy kaleidoscope (optional)
- student designs or other drawings or pictures

PLANNING AHEAD

You can either prepare each reflection station in advance, or set them up as the activity begins. In either case, the posterboard shouldn't be taped down, because students will want to move it to create different effects.

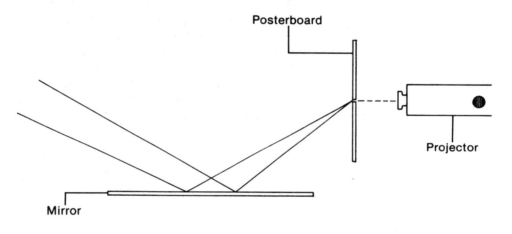

ACTIVITY

Begin by letting the students observe a reflection station for a few minutes to notice what is happening to the light. (Remember that the light is spreading, as well as being reflected, and students will probably notice this. Next, change the angle at which the light hits the mirror. (This can usually be done by moving the posterboard to the side.) Depending on the locations both of your light source and of the mirror, it may be necessary to move the light source to create a significantly different angle. The best results will be obtained when the room is dim, but not dark.

After students have experimented for a few minutes, stop to discuss what is happening. Begin the discussion by asking students to describe what they saw. Students should have noticed that the beam of light hit the mirror and bounced off. They should also have noticed that the angle at which the beam hit and bounced off changed as the posterboard, the mirror, or the light source was moved. In addition, students should notice that the beam of light spread out as it traveled across the desk. Ask students how the direction that the light hits the mirror will always affect the direction it bounces off. Allow students to observe some more as they arrive at their predictions.

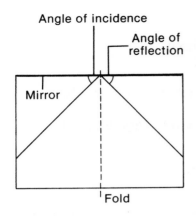

Angle of incidence

Angle of reflection

Mirror

Fold

Now, place a piece of paper on the table so the edge of the paper is flush with the mirror. Have someone (yourself or a student) trace one edge of the beam as it comes toward the mirror and then bounces off. (Be sure to trace only one edge of the beam and *its* reflection.) A ruler will provide a straight line.

The lines drawn on the paper and the line created by the base of the mirror represent the angle of incidence and the angle of reflection. Have students either fold their papers or cut out the angles and compare them by placing one piece on top of the other.

Ask students now to predict what will happen if the angle of the incoming light is changed, or if a second mirror is placed in the exiting light beam's path. Follow up such predictions with actual experiments by altering the angle or adding a hand-held mirror.

FURTHER EXPLORATION

As a follow-up activity, students can build simple kaleidoscopes. Students (with or without adult assistance) will need to take two small pieces of cardboard and cover them with either aluminum foil or metalized film, shiny side out. Hinge the two mirrors with tape. Now have students place a design or other drawing or picture on the desk and stand the kaleidoscope on top of it. Have the students experiment by changing the angle of the two mirrors and counting the number of images that can be seen. These homemade kaleidoscopes are safe and can be stored flat. If the classroom has a toy kaleidoscope, it can also be passed around for comparison.

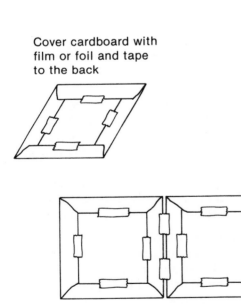

Cover cardboard with film or foil and tape to the back

Tape 2 mirrors together to form joint

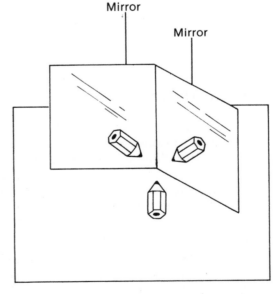

Mirror

Mirror

Adjust "mirror" angle to change the number of images seen.

Note: This is a good time to look at symmetry.

Rainbows

OVERVIEW

In this activity, students will make a rainbow and observe its properties. What causes a rainbow? As light travels through a prism (or raindrops), the light bends, and, as it bends, its wavelengths spread out. When the wavelengths spread out and become separated, our eyes see them as distinct colors. White light contains wavelengths of all these colors, but because they are mixed up and travel together, our eye sees this combination of all wavelengths as white.

Rainbows are not only fun to create, but they can also carry important scientific information. As a chemical burns, it gives off light. Some chemicals burn yellow, some green, and some blue, depending on the combination of frequencies in the light. By taking the light given off and separating it into a rainbow, one can easily see which frequencies are present and which are absent. This pattern of frequencies is as individual as a fingerprint, and can be used to identify that chemical in unknown burning substances. This process of identification is called spectroscopy.

MATERIALS

- a light source (such as a slide projector or the sun)
- a small piece of posterboard with a single, very narrow slit
- a small piece of posterboard with several tiny holes (optional)
- colored paper
- plain paper
- a prism
- plastic colored filters, colored transparent plastic report covers, or blank colored overhead transparencies in red, blue, and yellow

PLANNING AHEAD

If students are working indoors, set up your light source and attach the slit posterboard to it so that the light coming from the source is only a thin beam. This posterboard will control the light entering the prism. (The best rainbows are achieved with very thin slits. If the slit is too wide, only the edges of the image will have the rainbow effect while the middle will be mostly white light.)

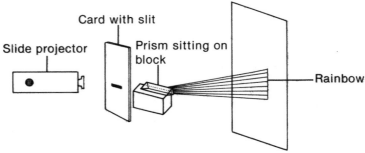

Card with slit

Slide projector

Prism sitting on block

Rainbow

ACTIVITY

Indoors, begin by demonstrating how to hold the prism in the beam of light so the rainbow is projected onto a wall or projection screen. To do this, hold the prism point down so that everyone can see. (If this activity is set up in a small learning center, a small rainbow is sufficient, and the prism can be held with the point up.) Outdoors, you may still need to use the posterboard with the slit to control the light entering the prism. The rainbow's location will be controlled by how the prism is held.

Give students a chance to play with the prism by moving it around and seeing how this affects the rainbow. For another interesting effect, you can switch the posterboard that has a single slit for one with several tiny holes. Now, instead of a single big rainbow, there are several little ones.

After every student has manipulated the prism, hold a class discussion. Ask: *How many colors did everyone see? Which color was on top and which was on the bottom? Where have you seen rainbows before? What did you think caused rainbows? Now, where do you think the colors come from? Do they come from the prism, or from the light?* Give students time to answer and to explain the reasons for their answers.

Next, place a piece of colored paper on the wall or screen where the rainbow is being projected. Students should be able to observe that the rainbow is still there. Then place a colored filter between the light and the prism. Students should observe that different parts of the rainbow will disappear.

Help students to realize that the color for the rainbow was in the light itself. Discuss how the order of the colors is always the same whether the rainbow is produced with a prism or appears after rain up in the sky. Then have students record the colors of the rainbow that they observed by drawing the rainbow on paper.

FURTHER EXPLORATION

Students can explore further with light and the color spectrum by seeing how mixing colors can produce new colors. (This will make clearer why green is always between blue and yellow on their rainbow.) To mix colors, have students use the red, blue, and yellow colored plastic filters, overlapping them and holding them up to light.

Opaque, Transparent, and Translucent

OVERVIEW

Light carries information in the form of images, brightness, and color. The terms opaque, transparent, and translucent all describe how much light can get through a material. Whenever light travels through something, some of the light is either absorbed or reflected back by the material. This prevents some information from reaching an observer.

In this experiment, students will put on puppet shows behind opaque, transparent, and translucent screens, and then discuss how much they knew about each show from what they were able to see.

The concepts of opacity, transparency, and translucency all come to mind when one thinks of a window. When you are looking out a window through a fairly clean piece of glass, a good deal of information about what is outside reaches your eyes through the transparent glass. If a sheer or translucent curtain is drawn across the window, much of your vision is obstructed. You would probably, however, be able to tell if it were midday, and could see the shadows of objects nearby, silhouetted on the curtain. When heavy, opaque curtains are drawn, all the visual information about what is going on outside the window is lost.

MATERIALS

- clothesline and clothespins
- puppets (They can either be made from a variety of materials or borrowed from an educational library to go with specific children's stories. For easy-to-make puppets, students can color and cut out various flat figures and attach popsicle sticks to have a way to hold on to them.)
- three boxes (optional)
- various transparent, translucent, and opaque objects (optional)

For the clear screen:

- a clear piece of plastic film or plexiglass (if it is warm outside, puppeteers and audience can be on opposite sides of a classroom window)

For the translucent screen:

- a light-colored bedsheet (if students are on both sides of a window, tape white tissue paper on the window instead)
- a lamp

For the opaque screen:

- a nonclear plastic tablecloth (if students are on two sides of a window, tape a few pieces of construction paper to the window instead)

PLANNING AHEAD

To set up screens, run a clothesline across the room and use tape or clothespins to attach the screens to the line.

ACTIVITY

This activity is best done with students working in small groups. Have students begin by creating a short play. You might suggest that they use a story they have read. If students are making their own puppets, have them embark on that project now. While students are making their puppets, either you or other students can easily set up the screens. After the puppets and screens are ready, give groups of students time to prepare their puppet shows to present to the class. Assign each group a particular screen to make sure that each screen is used for at least one performance.

When all the puppet shows have been presented, ask pairs of students to consider these questions: *Which puppet show was the easiest to understand? What screen let you know what colors the puppets were? What could you tell about the puppets when they were behind the partly-clear screen? What could you tell through the completely non-see-through screen?*

Students should now realize that the more light that came through a screen, the more information they got.

FURTHER EXPLORATION

Fill the three boxes with transparent, translucent, or opaque objects respectively. Label them accordingly, Transparent (Clear), Translucent (Partly Clear), and Opaque (Not Clear).

Have students discuss and then test the hypothesis that light brings information, by examining materials in the three boxes you have prepared, and deciding whether the materials have been sorted correctly.

Now have students come together to share their judgments about whether the items were correctly sorted. Since it may be difficult to make distinctions when sorting, accept all judgments. Students can also discuss how some translucent things let more light through than others. (For example, a piece of tissue paper lets more light through than a piece of typing paper.) You may want students to arrange the translucent items from those closest to transparent to those closest to opaque.